ATLANTIS AND OTHER LOST WORLDS

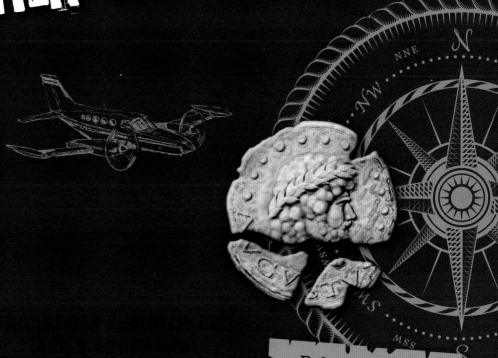

Robert Snedden

Gareth Stevens
PUBLISHING

Please visit our website, www.garethstevens.com.
For a free color catalog of all our high-quality books,
call toll free 1-800-542-2595 of fax 1-877-542-2596.

Cataloging-in-Publication Data

Names: Snedden, Robert.
Title: Atlantis and other lost worlds / Robert Snedden.
Description: New York : Gareth Stevens, 2017. | Series: Mystery hunters | Includes index.
Identifiers: ISBN 9781482459968 (pbk.) | ISBN 9781482459982 (library bound) | ISBN 9781482459975 (6 pack)
Subjects: LCSH: Atlantis (Legendary place)--Juvenile literature.
Classification: LCC GN751.S64 2017 | DDC 001.94--dc23

First Edition

Published in 2017 by
Gareth Stevens Publishing
111 East 14th Street, Suite 349
New York, NY 10003

Produced for Gareth Stevens by Calcium
Editors: Sarah Eason and Claudia Martin
Picture researcher: Rachel Blount
Designer: Emma DeBanks

Picture credits: Cover: Shutterstock: Linda Bucklin (bg), Panos Karas (bl), Jim Larkin (tr); Inside:
Library of Congress: George Grantham Bain Collection 20–21c; Shutterstock: Arfabita 37t,
Mila Atkovska 12–13b, AuntSpray 15t, George W. Bailey 10–11bg, Anton Balazh 22–23t, Arthur
Balitskiy 23, Boscorelli 22–23bg, Willyam Bradberry 12–13bg, Bukethun 20–21bg, Rachelle
Burnside 35b, Graham De'ath 35t, Dimitrios 8l, Joe Dunckley 34l, Eky studio 32–33bg, Everett –
Art 25t, Flashinmirror 40–41bg, Edward Haylan 28–29b, IndianSummer 10t, Kamonrat 26, Chris
Kolaczan 30, Vuk Kostic 9r, 34–35bg, Anna Kucherova 4–5 bg, Jim Larkin 1, Alberto Loyo 32b,
MSSA 18–19bg, Nagel Photography 5br, Jamen Percy 14–15bg, Photovolcanica.com 6–7bg,
Quick Shot 26–27bg, RS 16–17bg, Saiko3p 36–37bg, Sailorr 7tr, Semmick Photo38–39bg,
Science photo 8–9bg, 30–31 bg, Shyamalamuralinath 36b, Atelier Sommerland 10b, Jose Ignacio
Soto 24–25bg, Tolga Tezcan 5t, Victor Torres 24, Tuulijumala 12–13t, Vacclav 6–7b, Vibrant Image
Studio 28–29bg, WitR 38b, Yaalan 42–43bg, Gary Yim 33l; Wikimedia Commons: 14b, 16–17c,
George Grantham Bain, Library of Congress 17tr, Mattymoo101 21t, Maudslay 43, Dr. Konrad
Miller 29t, Thomas Murray 18l, NASA 39r, NASA, ESA and H.E. Bond (STScI) 42b, NASA/JPL-
Caltech 41b, Patrickneil 19, William Scott-Elliott (d 1930) 26–27b, Adalberto Hernandez Vega from
Copan Ruinas, Honduras 31t, Warofdreams 40.

Printed in China

CPSIA compliance information: Batch #CW17GS: For further information contact Gareth Stevens, New York, New York at 1-800-542-2595.

CONTENTS

Chapter 1

A WORLD OF IMAGINATION

People have always been fascinated by stories about lost cities and lands, of great cities that are impossible to find, of lands hidden beneath the surface of Earth, or kingdoms that have vanished beneath the ocean waves. Some people are so convinced by these tales that they believe they are more than just stories. They look for **evidence** that these lost places were real.

Unknown Lands

Why do we tell stories about **mythical** lost cities and lands? Tales of mysterious, distant places have always captured the imagination. Long before the map of the world was complete, it was easy to weave fantastic stories about what might lie in unknown parts of the planet. Until the seventeenth century, for example, the people of Europe had no idea that the continent of Australia even existed.

Some of the stories of lost places may be no more than that: just stories. However, **archaeologists** and scientists have uncovered evidence that some places that vanished from history actually did exist.

MYSTERY HUNTER

Look for the Mystery Hunter boxes throughout the book. They will ask you to consider the information given in each chapter and answer questions based on what you have read. Then turn to pages 44–45 to see if your answer is correct.

The Truth About Troy

You might have heard the story of the ancient city of Troy and its war with Greece, called the Trojan War, and how the Greeks soldiers hid in a giant wooden "horse" to get inside the enemy city. For a long time, historians believed that the story, like Troy itself, was just a myth.

The nineteenth-century German archaeologist Heinrich Schliemann thought the city really did exist. In a series of digs, Schliemann uncovered the ruins of Troy in what is now Turkey. The city does indeed seem to have been destroyed by the Greek armies of King Agamemnon sometime between 1260 and 1240 BC. However, the tale of the wooden horse may be no more than an exciting story.

Did the Greeks' wooden horse look something like this? No one knows!

MYSTERIOUS FACTS

Before Europeans arrived in America, Native Americans lived in towns and villages across the continent. In the southwestern United States, people lived in towns cut out of cliffs. Historians call these cliff dwellers "Pueblo peoples" (*pueblo* is Spanish for town). The largest cliff town was the "Cliff Palace" in Colorado. It was abandoned around AD 1300 and remained undiscovered until 1888, when riders looking for stray cattle came upon it.

The "Cliff Palace" was forgotten for 500 years.

Flood and Fire

Is it possible that natural disasters were the seeds for some of the myths and legends of lost places? Could floods, volcanic eruptions, or other disasters have buried whole cities beneath water or ash?

Lost in Legend

Legend tells us that the lost city of Ys, said to have been the most beautiful in Europe, once stood on the coast of Brittany in France. In one story, the coast was being worn away by the sea, threatening the city with flooding. The king built a wall around the city to protect it from the water. A single gate, to which only the king had the key, was opened at low tide to let ships in. One stormy night, however, the king's daughter was tempted by the Devil into opening the gate. The sea swept in and Ys was lost. According to the legend, the church bells of Ys can still be heard when the sea is calm.

It is easy to imagine how real experiences of flooding could give rise to a story like that of Ys. There are similar stories, such as the mythical city of Kitezh, which was said to have sunk beneath Lake Svetloyar in Russia. The Isles of Scilly off the coast of Cornwall in England are believed to be the site of the vanished great kingdom of Lyonesse—where the legendary King Arthur of Britain is said to have fought his last battle. In fact, there is some evidence that rising sea levels may have flooded large areas around AD 400 to 500, turning one large landmass into the many small islands we know today.

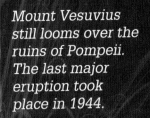

Mount Vesuvius still looms over the ruins of Pompeii. The last major eruption took place in 1944.

Lost Pompeii

An erupting volcano can also cause massive destruction. In AD 79, the volcano Vesuvius in Italy erupted in a devastating explosion that buried the Roman town of Pompeii under a thick layer of ash and rock. Pompeii vanished and became largely forgotten, except in stories. It was rediscovered nearly 1,700 years later, when a canal was being constructed near the site of the buried town.

Disaster came so swiftly to Pompeii that many people had no time to flee and were buried beneath the ash.

MYSTERY HUNTER

Until the ruins of Pompeii were discovered, the town was remembered mostly through stories and legends. Based on the information you have read about Pompeii, do you think it is possible that other lost worlds described in legends still lie hidden underground, waiting to be discovered? Give reasons for your answer.

Chapter 2

THE LEGEND OF ATLANTIS

The legend of the island of Atlantis is one of the longest lasting and best known of the "lost world" myths. The first record we have of the story comes from the Greek **philosopher** Plato, who wrote down the tale around 360 BC. Plato said Atlantis existed about 9,000 years before his own time, and that its story had been passed down through the centuries.

What Happened to Atlantis?

According to Plato, the founders of Atlantis were half god and half human. The island of Atlantis had mountains in the north and along the coast, and a great plain in the south that measured about 345 miles (555 km) by 230 miles (370 km). The capital city of Atlantis was said to have been carved from a mountain by the god Poseidon. It was set inside a series of circular canals, nested inside each other like a bull's-eye. A canal ran from the sea to the center of the city. The Atlanteans were a peaceful, wealthy people who had a lot of gold, silver, and other precious metals.

Plato told the story of how Atlantis was lost.

Going to War

According to the story, things began to go wrong when the Atlanteans grew greedy and wanted more and more riches. They built a large fleet of ships and set out to conquer the peoples of the Mediterranean. Only the city of Athens in Greece stood against them.

Finally, Zeus, king of the Greek gods, decided that the Atlanteans had become evil and had to be punished. He sent a series of terrible earthquakes that, over the course of a day and a night, sank mighty Atlantis beneath the waves of the Atlantic Ocean. According to the ancient Egyptians, it was impossible to sail across the ocean where Atlantis had been because of the mud left behind as the island sank.

The god Zeus, angered by the Atlanteans, decided to destroy them.

MYSTERIOUS FACTS

The ancient Greek port of Pavlopetri sank beneath 13 feet (4 m) of water 3,000 years ago, when earthquakes caused the land to shift. The city was rediscovered by archaeologists in 1967. Plato may have based the Atlantis legend on Pavlopetri.

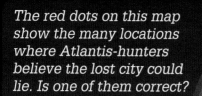

The red dots on this map show the many locations where Atlantis-hunters believe the lost city could lie. Is one of them correct?

Finding Atlantis

If Atlantis was an actual place, and not simply a myth, where might it have been? Over the centuries, many attempts have been made to pinpoint its location. Many "experts" on Atlantis have put forward reasons why it could have been just about anywhere in the world. The Atlantic Ocean, the Mediterranean and Caribbean Seas, Antarctica, Bolivia, Turkey, Germany— all have been suggested at one time or another.

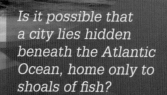

Is it possible that a city lies hidden beneath the Atlantic Ocean, home only to shoals of fish?

Atlantis in the Atlantic

Charles Orser, a historian at the New York State Museum, has said: "Pick a spot on the map, and someone has said that Atlantis was there. Every place you can imagine." Plato, however, was quite clear about where Atlantis was. As far as he was concerned, it lay in the Atlantic Ocean, out beyond the Strait of Gibraltar, which is the narrow stretch of sea that connects the Atlantic with the Mediterranean Sea. Yet, wherever Atlantis may have been, one thing is certain. It has never been found, other than in the imagination.

For thousands of years after Plato wrote his account, it was easy to believe all kinds of things might be hidden beneath the surface of the ocean. No one could go down and take a look, after all! However, now we have submarines and **sonar** that can map the ocean floor. It is almost impossible to believe that the remains of an entire island civilization have never been found. According to what scientists now understand about the processes that shape Earth, it is also impossible that there was once a landmass of the size that Plato describes out in the middle of the Atlantic Ocean.

Spanish Findings

In 2011, Hartford University professor Richard Freund announced that, using satellite imagery and **ground-penetrating radar**, he had found Atlantis, or at least Atlantean cities. He claimed the city was buried beneath swampy land north of Cádiz in southern Spain. Spanish scientists dismiss Freund's claims as "sensationalist" and "fanciful." There is no doubt that there really is an archaeological site waiting to be excavated and explored near Cádiz, but few people believe that it really is Atlantis.

The Thera Eruption

By 5,000 years ago, the Minoans on the island of Crete in the Mediterranean Sea had formed one of the world's first great civilizations. They were the first Europeans to have a written language. They built impressive palaces and paved roads. They created a powerful navy of ships. Then a terrible disaster brought about the collapse of the Minoan civilization. Could the Minoans have been the inspiration for Atlantis?

The Destruction of Santorini

Today, the Greek island of Santorini is the biggest of a group of islands to the north of Crete. Just over 3,500 years ago, however, this island group was one large island named Thera. It was home to the Minoan city of Akrotiri. Around 1600 BC, Akrotiri was shaken by a massive earthquake. This was followed by a huge volcanic eruption, one of the largest in human history, which blew out the center of Thera. It has been estimated that 10 million tons (9 million t) of rock, ash, and gases were blasted 25 miles (40 km) into the air.

These are the remains of the great Minoan palace at Knossos in Crete.

Today, the center of ancient Thera is filled by the sea.

Tsunami Disaster

The force of the eruption triggered a **tsunami** that caused flooding and devastation when it struck the Minoan cities on the coast of Crete. It is believed that Greeks from the mainland then took advantage of the Minoans' weakened state, and launched an invasion.

The Start of a Legend

Does this account remind you of Plato's story that the Athenians fought against the Atlanteans? Of course, Plato said that Atlantis had fallen some 9,000 years before his time, while the eruption of Thera and fall of the Minoans had actually happened around 1,200 years earlier. It is quite likely, however, that Plato knew only that the disaster had happened long ago and had no clear idea exactly when.

There is no firm evidence that Plato used the Minoan disaster as a basis for his Atlantis story. However, one thing we can say for certain is that the disaster was a real event that had a long-lasting effect on the way civilization developed around the Mediterranean Sea.

MYSTERY HUNTER

Do you think Atlantis was a real place? Do you think the myth is based on real events? How likely does it seem to you that Plato based his story on the fate of the Minoans? Look again at the information you have read and give reasons for your answers.

Chapter 3

HOLLOW EARTH

Underground kingdoms make an appearance in the traditional stories of many peoples. Several religions talk about an underworld where lost souls are sent forever. The idea that Earth is a hollow sphere was quite widely believed in the nineteenth and early twentieth centuries. Even today, some people believe that cities or whole civilizations might be hidden beneath our planet's surface.

Polar Openings

In 1818, U.S. army officer John Cleves Symmes (1780–1829) suggested that there were openings to the inner Earth at the poles. At this point, no one had visited either pole. Symmes suggested that a ship sailing through a hole at the North Pole would sail over the rim and onto an ocean on the inside of Earth, with its masts pointing toward the center of the planet, rather than toward the sky. His ideas started to gain popularity.

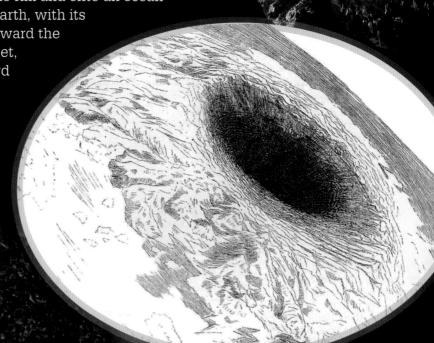

Symmes believed a hole at the North Pole led into Earth's interior.

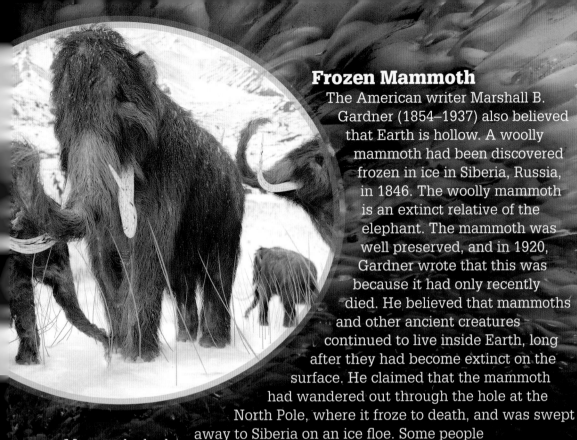

Frozen Mammoth

The American writer Marshall B. Gardner (1854–1937) also believed that Earth is hollow. A woolly mammoth had been discovered frozen in ice in Siberia, Russia, in 1846. The woolly mammoth is an extinct relative of the elephant. The mammoth was well preserved, and in 1920, Gardner wrote that this was because it had only recently died. He believed that mammoths and other ancient creatures continued to live inside Earth, long after they had become extinct on the surface. He claimed that the mammoth had wandered out through the hole at the North Pole, where it froze to death, and was swept away to Siberia on an ice floe. Some people found Gardner's ideas convincing.

Mammoths had long tusks.

Tall Tales

In 1908, the American **novelist** Willis George Emerson (1856–1918) published a book called *The Smoky God*. The book claimed to be the true story of Olaf Jansen, a Norwegian sailor. In the book, Jansen's ship sails through a hole near the North Pole, which leads to Earth's interior. For two years, Jansen lives with 12-foot-tall (3.6 m) people in an underground world that is lit by a central sun. Emerson wrote that this people's capital city was the Garden of Eden, home to Earth's first people. Most people saw the book for what it was, an exciting work of fiction, but others took it as further proof of a hollow Earth.

In 1864, the French writer Jules Verne (1828–1905) wrote his famous book *Journey to the Center of the Earth*, which tells of explorers traveling through volcanic tubes into the interior of Earth. There, they discover prehistoric animals and an underground ocean. However, Verne never pretended that his tale was anything more than just an adventure story.

Shambhala

In 1933, the British author James Hilton (1900–1954) wrote a story about a valley called Shangri-La, hidden in the Himalaya Mountains in Tibet. He wrote that it was inhabited by happy people who live for thousands of years. Hilton based his story on a much older one— that of the mysterious city of Shambhala.

The Forbidden Land

The mythical paradise of Shambhala (or Shamballa) has been given many names: the Forbidden Land, the Land of White Waters, the Land of Living Fire, and the Land of Wonders, among others. Hindus have known it as the land from which the Vedas, their oldest **scriptures**, come. The Chinese know it as Hsi Tien, the Western Paradise that is the home of the mother goddess Xi Wangmu. But throughout Asia it is best known by its **Sanskrit** name, Shambhala, which means "the place of peace."

When Europeans and Americans started to hear stories about Shambhala in the nineteenth century, they were fascinated. Some said that Shambhala was the city of Agartha, a land of advanced people hidden inside Earth. The scientific knowledge and skills of the people of Agartha were supposedly far greater than that of the people who live on Earth's surface. According to some stories, their knowledge is based on technology from Atlantis, carried into Earth by people fleeing the destruction of their land.

This painting shows the Buddha enthroned in paradise. Shambhala is said to be the ancient home of the Buddha.

Explorer Richard Byrd gets ready to take flight.

Admiral Byrd

Admiral Richard E. Byrd (1888–1957) of the U.S. Navy was an explorer who flew to the North Pole in 1926 and over the South Pole in 1929. Rumors sprang up that Byrd kept a secret diary. It supposedly describes how he flew into the hollow interior of Earth, traveling over mountains, lakes, and rivers and eventually reaching cities. There, he was met by strange flying machines that took him to a meeting with the king and queen of Agartha. No evidence has ever been found to back up the story of the secret diary—but some people claim that is because it has been hidden by the U.S. government!

Hollow Earth Science

Over the centuries, scientists, explorers, and thinkers have worked to improve their understanding of our planet and the forces that shape it. Scientists look for ways to explain what they see around them, putting forward theories that can be tested by experiments and observations. For example, in 1692 the British astronomer Edmund Halley (1656–1742) attempted to explain the movements of a compass needle by suggesting Earth was hollow.

Spinning Shells

Halley is best known today for figuring out the orbit of the **comet** that is named for him, but he had many other interests. He suggested that Earth was formed of a series of hollow shells. The shells nested inside each other like Russian dolls. Each shell rotated at a different speed and had its own magnetic poles. It was the constantly changing positions of these poles that affected the compass needle.

Sir Edmund Halley was a respected astronomer.

Two Tiny Suns

The Scottish **physicist** Sir John Leslie (1766–1832) is best remembered for his groundbreaking research into heat. However, in his 1829 book *Elements of Natural Philosophy*, he also suggested that Earth is hollow. Some later writers took the idea further and claimed that Leslie had suggested that there were two little suns inside Earth. They were named Pluto and Proserpina.

Antigravity?

There is one big problem with the idea of people living inside a hollow Earth. That problem is gravity. Gravity is the force that holds us on to the surface of the planet, pulling us in toward the center of Earth. What would hold you to Earth if you were standing on the inside of the planet? People who believe in the idea of a hollow Earth claim that the planet's center of gravity is just a few hundred miles beneath the surface, rather than at the center. In scientific terms, we now know this to be untrue.

John Quincy Adams became president in 1825.

MYSTERIOUS FACTS

Some people claim that U.S. President John Quincy Adams (1767–1848) believed Earth is hollow. They point out that he approved a polar expedition that believers in a hollow Earth hoped would find a hidden entrance. Historians say there is no proof that Adams thought the expedition would succeed; he just wanted to support the exploration of unknown regions. The expedition was canceled by the next president.

A Universe Inside?

One interesting theory is that we are all, right now, living on the inside of Earth—and that we are looking in, not out, at the rest of the universe. Outside, there is nothing. Cyrus Teed, a doctor from New York State, proposed such a hollow Earth in 1869. In 1870, Teed changed his name to Koresh and started a new religious movement called Koreshanity, based on his outside-in universe ideas. He attracted some 4,000 believers.

The Rectilineator

Teed called his idea "Cellular Cosmogony." He was determined to prove his idea scientifically and built a device he called the "rectilineator." This was supposed to demonstrate that the surface of Earth is concave, curving inward, as it would be if we were on the inside of a sphere. Teed was pleased with the results of his experiments, but today's scientists believe his equipment was flawed and there were errors in his measurements.

Cyrus Teed carried out many experiments to try to prove his theories.

Could It Be True?

Of course, the idea of the entire universe being held inside Earth is nonsense. Isn't it? H.S.M. Coxeter (1907–2003) was one of the twentieth century's most respected geometers. A geometer is a mathematician who focuses on geometry, which is the study of shapes, size, and spaces.

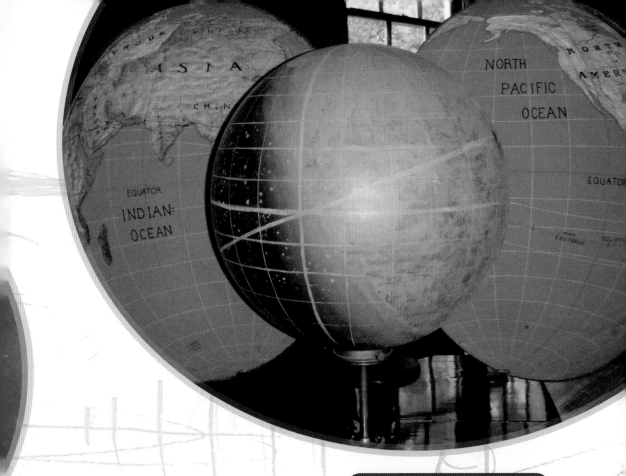

This is a model of Teed's hollow Earth, complete with continents and the universe on the inside!

Essentially, Coxeter suggested, geometry can be used to show that the universe-inside-Earth idea is actually possible. He said, "Any observation we can make on the outside of Earth has an exact duplicate version inside. There would be no way to tell which was the truth."

In 1992, the famous mathematician Martin Gardner (1914–2010) said that most mathematicians think it is impossible to disprove "an inside-out Universe, with properly adjusted physical laws."

MYSTERY HUNTER

What do you think? Can it really be possible that we, and the whole universe, are inside a hollow sphere? Look at the text again and give reasons for your answer.

Chapter 4

LOST LANDS

During the nineteenth century, it was not unusual for scientists to suggest that land bridges and even whole continents had disappeared beneath the oceans. This seemed like a reasonable way to explain how similar **species** of plants and animals could be found in different places in the world, separated by vast oceans.

Land Bridges

Land bridges are not a myth. A land bridge is a stretch of land that links one continent or island with another. They appear and disappear as sea levels rise and fall. For example, thousands of years ago, the Bering land bridge linked Asia with North America across what is now the Bering Strait near Alaska. It allowed people to cross from Asia into the Americas for the first time, around 20,000 years ago. The land bridge was submerged as sea levels rose about 15,000 years ago at the end of the last ice age.

Drifting Continents

If land bridges are real, what about disappearing continents? Modern geology tells us that, over the course of millions of years, the continents have drastically changed their shapes and positions. This is the theory of plate tectonics, or continental drift, which says that Earth's crust is broken up into a number of large pieces, called plates. These plates float slowly around on the molten interior of the planet. It is the movement of these plates that causes earthquakes and volcanoes, pushes up mountains, and opens out oceans.

New Zealand is today nearly all that remains of Zealandia.

There is evidence that the movement of the plates has caused parts of continents to sink beneath the oceans. For example, Zealandia was once part of the same supercontinent as Australia. Most of Zealandia had sunk beneath the Pacific Ocean by 23 million years ago. Today, just New Zealand and a few other islands are above the surface. Such evidence has encouraged some people to hope there may be much larger submerged continents. However, geologists believe there are no more large surprises lying beneath the waves.

225 million years ago

150 million years ago

65 million years ago

Present day

MYSTERIOUS FACTS

These diagrams show how the continents have moved and changed.

The idea of continental drift was first suggested by German scientist Alfred Wegener (1880–1930) in 1912:

- Wegener first developed his theory of continental drift by cutting out maps of the continents and fitting them together like a jigsaw puzzle. By doing so, he formed one giant continent, called a supercontinent.

- Wegener called his supercontinent Pangaea. Scientists now believe that a supercontinent really did exist 300 million years ago, before it slowly broke up to form the present-day continents.

- Wegener was mocked for his ideas. He didn't live to see the evidence that proved he was right, from studies of the ocean floor to **fossil** findings.

23

Mu, a Lost Continent

In the nineteenth century, an amateur archaeologist named Augustus Le Plongeon (1825–1908) came up with the idea of a continent hidden beneath the waves of the Pacific Ocean. He called it Mu. Plongeon got his idea while visiting the ruins of Chichén Itzá in Yucatán, Mexico, once home to the Maya people. His proof was his own translation of a Mayan book called the Troano **Codex**. One problem was that he was not a very skilled translator: some of what he thought was writing was actually part of an ornamental design!

The Maya built huge stepped pyramids like this one, at Chichén Itzá.

Queen Moo

In a book called *Queen Moo and the Egyptian Sphinx*, published in 1896, Le Plongeon claimed that the Troano Codex revealed that the Maya were the **ancestors** of the ancient Egyptians. He also believed that the Maya were the survivors of a disaster that had destroyed the ancient continent of Mu. Le Plongeon thought that Mu was actually Atlantis, and that "Queen Moo" of Atlantis had founded the ancient Egyptian civilization.

The Troano Codex inspired Le Plongeon's theories about Mu.

The Naacal Brotherhood

The story of the lost civilization of Mu became popular in 1931, when Colonel James Churchward (1851–1936) published a book called *The Lost Continent of Mu*. He claimed that Mu had stretched across the Pacific Ocean from north of Hawaii to Easter Island, over 4,000 miles (6,400 km) to the south. Churchward said that Mu was an advanced civilization of 64 million people that had been wiped out by an earthquake, sinking beneath the Pacific Ocean 12,000 years ago. Atlantis, a **colony** of Mu, was destroyed in the same way 1,000 years later. All the world's major ancient civilizations, according to Churchward, had grown from colonies of Mu.

Churchward claimed he learned all this in India, when he became friendly with a priest who told him he was one of the only survivors of the "Naacal Brotherhood," which started on Mu 70,000 years ago. Although Churchward was never able to produce evidence to back up his claims, his books are still read today. Some people believe that Australia was part of the continent of Mu. This has led to attempts to find evidence of the people of Mu along the coasts of Australia. Perhaps unsurprisingly, no trace has been found.

Lemuria, the Missing Link

In 1864, the English **zoologist**
Philip Sclater (1829–1913) was
studying lemurs (tree-dwelling
mammals) in Madagascar, an island off
the coast of Africa. He was interested by
the fact that very similar species exist
all the way across the Indian Ocean
in India. He suggested that the Indian
and Madagascan animals might have
evolved together on a continent
that had since vanished beneath
the Indian Ocean. He called this
lost continent Lemuria.

Evolution Island

To Sclater, a missing
continent was a good
way to explain the
similarities between
animals on opposite
sides of an ocean. At
this time, scientists were
becoming familiar with
Charles Darwin's theory of
evolution, published in 1859.
According to Darwin, all living
things share a common ancestor, but
changed over the course of millions of
years, to give rise to the huge variety of
species we see in the world today.

*The origins of
lemurs like these
fascinated Sclater.*

Getting Stranger

Ernst Haeckel (1834–1919), a German **naturalist**, had similar ideas to Sclater. He suggested there must once have been a land bridge across the Indian Ocean, linking Madagascar to India. Going further, Haeckel also claimed that lemurs were the ancestors of the human race and that his lost land bridge was the "cradle of the human race."

Helena Blavatsky (1831–1891) went even further. In her book *The Secret Doctrine*, published in 1888, she claimed that "Lemuria" had once been the home of egg-laying beings with jelly-like bodies. A third eye gave them mind-reading abilities. There is, of course, not a shred of evidence for these claims!

Drifting Apart

Scientists abandoned the idea of a vanished land bridge or continent in the Indian Ocean when the theory of continental drift was widely accepted in the early twentieth century. Scientists now believe that Madagascar and India were once part of the Gondwanaland supercontinent. The supercontinent broke apart, rather than sank, 88 million years ago.

This nineteenth-century map shows "hidden" landmasses in red.

MYSTERIOUS FACTS

In 1999, a research ship drilling in the Indian Ocean discovered evidence that a large island had been submerged by rising sea levels around 20 million years ago. Samples of pollen and wood recovered from the seabed, today called the Kerguelen Plateau, showed that it must once have been above the surface. Although the plateau is three times bigger than Japan, it is not large enough to have been a link between India and Madagascar.

Hyperborea, Land of the Far North

The ancient Greeks told stories about a beautiful land far to the north, called Hyperborea. According to the stories, if you traveled far enough north, you would eventually leave behind the lands of cold winters. There lay Hyperborea, where it was always spring and the sun shone 24 hours a day.

Beyond the North Wind

According to the legend, Hyperborea was bordered in the north by a river that encircled Earth, and in the south by great mountain peaks. These mountains were the home of the god of the north wind, Boreas, who brought winter to the lands of the south. The name Hyperborea means "beyond the north wind." The people of Hyperborea lived peaceful lives, untroubled by old age and disease. Was Hyperborea just a story, or was the myth based on descriptions of real places visited by Greek travelers?

Where Is Hyperborea?

At different times, different Greek writers gave a range of locations for Hyperborea. In the early days of their civilization, the Greeks believed the wind god Boreas lived in Thrace, a region between modern Greece and Turkey. After the fourth century BC, some writers identified Hyperborea with Britain. They wrote of Britain's "unusually temperate climate" and of a "notable temple... spherical in shape," which some people believe is Stonehenge.

Was Stonehenge a Hyperborean temple?

Land of the Midnight Sun

The fact that the sun shines 24 hours a day in Hyperborea suggests a location inside the Arctic Circle, which would count out Britain as a location. North of the Arctic Circle, the sun remains above the horizon for 24 hours on at least one day of the year. This is often called the "Midnight Sun."

The Greeks were certainly aware that the farther from the equator you travel, the shorter the summer nights become. Around 325 BC, the Greek explorer Pytheas of Massalia sailed around Britain. It is not certain how far north Pytheas traveled: he may have reached Iceland or Norway—though he failed to find Hyperborea. He gave the earliest recorded description of the Midnight Sun and polar ice.

This copy of a Greek map shows the extent of the world the Greeks knew during the second century AD.

MYSTERY HUNTER

Do you think that the theory of continental drift might encourage people to believe in the idea of sunken, lost worlds? Give reasons for your answer.

Chapter 5

HIDDEN CITIES

For centuries, travelers took home tales of mysterious cities of power and wealth. Some of these tales may have been nothing more than stories designed to amuse and dazzle, but some of them may have been true.

Abandoned Tikal

Some ancient cities have disappeared from view for centuries. Tikal was an important city of the Maya Empire in what is now Guatemala. When the city flourished, between AD 600 and 890, it had a number of pyramid temples, the largest of which stood 215 feet (65 m) tall. Yet by AD 1000, the city was abandoned. For hundreds of years it remained largely unknown, although stories were still told about it. It was not until 1848 that the first explorers visited Tikal.

Much of Tikal was swallowed by the forest.

City of the Monkey God

The legend of the City of the
Monkey God, also known as the
White City (Ciudad Blanca),
began with American explorer
Theodore Morde (1911–1954).
In 1940, Morde claimed he had
found the ruins of a great city
in Honduras, and brought back
evidence such as stone tools. However,
he never gave the exact location of his city.
In 2015, researchers found ruins in the rain forests
of Honduras. Many archaeologists are skeptical
that the ruins are of Morde's lost great city.
They believe that there were many small towns
scattered around the area and that the City of the
Monkey God was, and still is, a myth.

*Was there really a
City of the Monkey
God, or is it just
a legend?*

The Lost Oasis

In stories, Zerzura is a lost city in the Libyan desert. At the start
of the twentieth century, the Libyan desert was almost entirely
unmapped. In the 1920s and 1930s, expeditions to find Zerzura
changed that. They also uncovered a treasure trove, not of gold,
but of knowledge. Evidence was found of previously unknown
ancient peoples who had lived in the area before it became desert.
Explorers also learned new desert travel techniques. One explorer,
Ralph Bagnold (1896–1990), carried out research into how sand
dunes were formed. But, of Zerzura, there has never been a trace.

MYSTERIOUS FACTS

The village of Atlit-Yam lies about half
a mile (1 km) off the coast of Israel, at
the bottom of the Mediterranean Sea.
Dating from 7000 BC, it is one of the
oldest known sunken settlements. It is
so well preserved that the remains of
beetles called weevils have been found
in its grain stores.

El Dorado, Legendary City of Gold

Since the sixteenth century, soon after the Spanish and other Europeans first arrived in the Americas, explorers have searched for El Dorado, the legendary lost "City of Gold." It is easy to see why a city filled with gold would attract the attention of fortune-hunters. Many expeditions have set off into the mountains and forests of Central and South America, and all have failed to find the golden city. El Dorado is still a legend, still just a dream of wealth.

The Origins of El Dorado

To find out how the El Dorado legend began, we have to investigate the Muisca tribe of Colombia in South America. This tribe lived over 1,000 years ago in the area where Colombia's capital, Bogotá, is now.

Whenever the Muisca appointed a new king, they carried out a special ritual. The new leader was stripped naked and covered in gold dust. He stepped onto a highly decorated raft with his attendants and heaps of gold and other treasures, and was paddled into the middle of a **sacred** lake. There, the king would jump into the water to wash the gold dust from his body, while his attendants threw the treasures into the lake as an offering to the gods.

The Muisca performed their ceremonies on Lake Guatavita.

The Gilded One

To the Muisca, "El Dorado" was not a city. Their new king, covered in gold dust, was El Dorado—"the Gilded One." For the Muisca, gold did not mean wealth: it was an offering to the gods. But for the people arriving from Europe, it meant great wealth indeed.

Hearing the story of the gold in the lake, the Spanish were unable to believe that so much gold had been, in their eyes, simply thrown away. A legend soon began to grow of a magnificent golden city. A Spanish army traveled to the homeland of the Muisca in 1537. It was a long and difficult journey, and many soldiers died along the way. When they finally reached their destination, they were astonished by the skill of the Muisca in crafting objects from gold. They had seen nothing like it in Europe. However, there was no city of gold.

The Muisca were skilled workers of gold for figures, masks, and jewelry.

Searching for Camelot

Camelot is the city of the legendary King Arthur of Britain, where he and his knights met around the famous Round Table. But did it really exist? And did Arthur exist? Many suggestions have been made as to where Camelot might have been located. Some are more convincing than others.

Caerleon

One suggestion for the site of Camelot is Caerleon, in Wales. This was one of three Roman legionary forts in Britain (the name Caerleon comes from the Latin words for "fortress" and "legion"). Many historians believe the legends of King Arthur may be based on a **Romano-British** leader who fought the **Anglo-Saxons** invading Britain in the fifth and sixth centuries AD. As the Anglo-Saxons pushed the Britons back into what is now Wales, locating Camelot there would make sense.

Cadbury Castle

Another possibility is Cadbury Castle, a fort built on a hill in Somerset, England, around 500 BC. Researchers have uncovered evidence that the fort's defenses were strengthened during the period of the Anglo-Saxon invasions. It was also larger than other forts of the time, which suggests that it was the home of a ruler of some kind. According to legend, the hill fort is hollow and Arthur and his knights sleep there until they are needed again.

The hill fort at Cadbury is the mound in the background of this photograph.

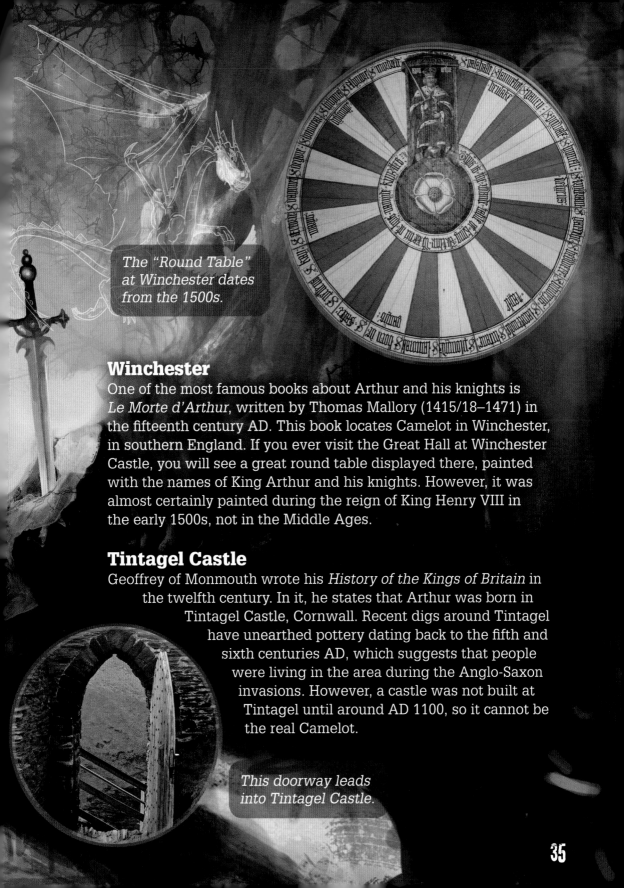

The "Round Table" at Winchester dates from the 1500s.

Winchester

One of the most famous books about Arthur and his knights is *Le Morte d'Arthur*, written by Thomas Mallory (1415/18–1471) in the fifteenth century AD. This book locates Camelot in Winchester, in southern England. If you ever visit the Great Hall at Winchester Castle, you will see a great round table displayed there, painted with the names of King Arthur and his knights. However, it was almost certainly painted during the reign of King Henry VIII in the early 1500s, not in the Middle Ages.

Tintagel Castle

Geoffrey of Monmouth wrote his *History of the Kings of Britain* in the twelfth century. In it, he states that Arthur was born in Tintagel Castle, Cornwall. Recent digs around Tintagel have unearthed pottery dating back to the fifth and sixth centuries AD, which suggests that people were living in the area during the Anglo-Saxon invasions. However, a castle was not built at Tintagel until around AD 1100, so it cannot be the real Camelot.

This doorway leads into Tintagel Castle.

Dvãrakã, the City of Krishna

Dvãrakã, "the many-gated city," is said to have been named by the Hindu god Krishna. It is one of the "seven sacred cities" of Hinduism. Until the twentieth century, no one thought that stories about Dvãrakã might be based on a real city.

Crystal Palaces

According to Hindu tradition, the city's parks and gardens were filled with the sounds of birds and bees. There were 900,000 royal palaces, built of crystal and silver and decorated with huge emeralds. The streets were kept cool by being sprinkled with water, and were shaded by banners waving from flagpoles. Lord Krishna lived in a particularly beautiful private area, surrounded by the 16,000 palaces of his queens.

Legend has it that, when Krishna left Earth to return to his heavenly home, the city of Dvãrakã sank beneath the sea. According to an ancient Indian text:

"The sea, which had been beating against the shores, suddenly broke the boundary that was imposed on it by nature. The sea rushed into the city. It coursed through the streets of the beautiful city... I saw the beautiful buildings becoming submerged one by one. In a matter of a few moments it was all over... There was no trace of the city. Dvãrakã was just a name; just a memory."

The god Krishna is said to have lived in Dvãrakã.

Finding Dvãrakã?

Like many other legendary
cities, Dvãrakã was thought to be
no more than a myth. However, in
1963, investigations were carried out at
the present-day city of Dwarka, on the coast
of India. Researchers found evidence that
suggested there had been a settlement there as early
as 1500 BC. Archaeologists later explored under
the sea too, and discovered what might be stone
blocks from ancient walls 130 feet (40 m) beneath
the surface. Some researchers believe these are just
natural rock formations. However, others believe the
rocks suggest there may be some historical basis for
the city of Dvãrakã.

*The present-day
Indian city of
Dwarka is a port.*

MYSTERY HUNTER

Looking again at the information you have read,
why do you think there have been so many
stories of lost cities that have been swallowed
by the sea? Give reasons for your answer.

Chapter 6
STRANGE UNIVERSE

When faced with only partly understood ideas, many people are more than willing to let their imaginations fill in the gaps in their knowledge. And what could be less understood than the huge Universe? The Universe is so vast that there are almost certainly other intelligent life-forms somewhere out there. But is there any evidence that they have already visited us?

Ancient Astronauts

In the 1970s, the idea that Earth had been visited in the past by space travelers from other worlds gained some popularity. The believers said that alien astronauts had helped humans with feats of engineering that would have been beyond us, such as building the pyramids in Egypt. No convincing evidence was brought forward to support the idea that aliens have ever visited Earth. In fact, some of the "evidence" in the form of ancient pottery that was supposed to show flying saucers has been proven to be fake! Historians can also tell us roughly how the pyramids were built, using human intelligence and labor, sleds, and ramps.

Were we smart enough to build the pyramids ourselves, or did we need alien help?

Apollo astronaut Buzz Aldrin stands on the moon.

Trip to the Far Side

Our moon keeps nearly the same face turned toward Earth all the time. It is impossible to see most of the far side of the moon unless you go there. Not surprisingly, this has led people to wonder what might be on the far side.

Some people have suggested that the U.S. astronauts who visited the moon between 1968 and 1972 saw evidence of aliens there, including UFOs and even a moon base. There were also some people who claimed to see alien structures in photographs sent back from the moon, including a mile-wide pyramid on the far side in a photograph from the 1972 Apollo 17 mission. These people claim that the U.S. government instructed the astronauts to keep quiet about it.

The U.S. space agency, the National Aeronautics and Space Administration (NASA), states that all of these claims are **hoaxes**, misunderstandings, or just wishful thinking. The more detailed photographs of the moon returned from later probes, such as the *Lunar Reconnaissance Orbiter*, launched in 2009, show no sign of alien objects at all.

MYSTERIOUS FACTS

No evidence has been found for life on another planet. But the Kepler Space Observatory was launched in 2009 to find planets that might be habitable:

- By 2016, Kepler had found more than 2,000 planets outside our solar system, orbiting other suns.

- Of those planets, more than 40 are in the "habitable zone" of their sun. In the habitable zone, the temperature is just right to allow liquid water to exist. Liquid water is essential for life.

39

Life on Mars?

For at least 100 years, people have thought, and sometimes worried, about the possibility of life on Mars. In 1898, H.G. Wells (1866–1946) wrote the novel *The War of the Worlds* about an invasion from Mars. The story has been popular ever since, and it has been made into several movies, a TV series, a radio program, and video games.

Martian Canals

Wells was inspired by reports that astronomer Percival Lowell (1855–1916) had used a telescope to see features on Mars that he thought could be canals built by Martians. Other astronomers were skeptical, but the idea captured the public imagination. The existence of canals on Mars was finally disproved after the first space probes reached the planet in 1965.

However, no matter how detailed our view of Mars has become, there are still people who claim to see extraordinary things there, including a giant stone face and pyramids. Could that be possible?

H.G. Wells imagined a Martian invasion of Earth.

The Face on Mars

The "face" on Mars was first seen in an image captured by the *Viking 1* orbiter in 1976. The *Viking* chief scientist called it "a trick of light and shadow." Later Mars missions sent back more detailed images of the feature and most people now accept that the face was an optical illusion. The so-called "pyramids" can be explained in the same way. Other features on Mars have been said to resemble Mickey Mouse, Kermit the Frog, and a smiley face!

Seeing Things?

In January 2015, it was claimed by UFO researchers that the *Curiosity* rover, then exploring the surface of Mars, had captured the shadow of a human-like life-form on the planet. The photograph in question had been taken by the rover in 2012 and had been available for anyone to see on NASA's website since then. If genuine photographic evidence of **humanoid** life on Mars had been made public for over two years, surely more fuss would have been made about it?

Some people have claimed to see strange things in the shadows cast by the Curiosity *rover.*

It Came from Outer Space

In 2012, NASA had to deal with thousands of inquiries from people who were concerned that a rogue planet called Nibiru was approaching Earth and threatening to destroy our world. NASA responded that such claims were an Internet hoax and "ludicrous." But where did the idea come from?

Return of the Ancient Astronauts

According to a 1976 book by writer Zecharia Sitchin (1920–2010), ancient Sumerian tablets from around 5,000 years ago tell of a planet named Nibiru. Sitchin wrote that Nibiru travels on a long orbit through the solar system that takes it out beyond Neptune and then inward, to pass near Earth every 3,600 years or so. Nibiru, according to Sitchin, was inhabited by an intelligent race of aliens that created humans through **genetic engineering**.

A Tangled Conspiracy

In 1995, a woman named Nancy Lieder claimed to have received a warning from aliens that a "Planet X" was going to travel through the inner solar system in 2003, causing a catastrophe that would wipe out all human civilization. When (not surprisingly) 2003 passed without calamity, Lieder said she had told a "white lie"— Planet X really was coming, but she refused to say when.

It wasn't long before Lieder's Planet X and Sitchin's Nibiru became linked in people's minds, although Sitchin denied there was any connection between his work and Lieder's claims.

There are many catastrophe theories based around large objects hitting Earth. Some people believe the star Monocerotis (right) is on a collision course with Earth.

This Mayan inscription gives a date in December 2012.

There was another surge of interest in Nibiru in 2012, when it was linked to supposed predictions made by the ancient Maya that the world would end in that year.

Scientist David Morrison of NASA hoped that when Nibiru failed to appear in 2012, it would encourage people to use "rational thought and baloney detection." However, he doubted that would happen.

Is the Truth Out There?

What is really interesting about the Nibiru story, and about so many other stories of lost cities and lands, is what it tells us about ourselves. Why are so many people prepared to suspend their disbelief and accept such tales when there is no hard evidence? Perhaps the Nibiru story also reminds us that a good mystery hunter should weigh up all the evidence before jumping to any conclusions. What do you think?

MYSTERY HUNTER

Why do you think some people believe in **conspiracy theories** and think that governments or organizations such as NASA might want to keep the truth from them? Give reasons for your answers.

MYSTERY HUNTER ANSWERS

Chapter 1

Q Until the ruins of Pompeii were discovered, the town was remembered mostly through stories and legends. Based on the information you have read about Pompeii, do you think it is possible that other lost worlds described in legends still lie hidden underground, waiting to be discovered? Give reasons for your answer.

A It is quite probable that there are other cities or villages waiting to be discovered. Volcanic eruptions, mudslides, or just the passing of time could have buried many settlements. Although the likelihood of finding a city as large and well preserved as Pompeii is now small, archaeologists do still frequently make new discoveries.

Chapter 2

Q Do you think Atlantis was a real place? Do you think the myth is based on real events? How likely does it seem to you that Plato based his story on the fate of the Minoans? Look again at the information you have read and give reasons for your answers.

A What we know of the Minoans, who built a largely peaceful civilization destroyed by a natural disaster, fits well into the Atlantis story. It would seem very likely that Plato was inspired by the fate of the Minoans, but we'll never know for sure. Perhaps he was inspired by other stories of earthquakes and disaster. The story of Atlantis may just be an enjoyable myth.

Chapter 3

Q Can it really be possible that we, and the whole Universe, are inside a hollow sphere? What do you think? Give reasons for your answer.

A There is no way to prove beyond doubt that we are not in a hollow sphere, as we can only make scientific judgments about what we can test, measure, or calculate for ourselves. Most scientists find the idea of an inside-out Universe unlikely.

Chapter 4

Q *Do you think that the theory of continental drift might encourage people to believe in the idea of sunken, lost worlds? Give reasons for your answer.*

A The theory of continental drift tells us that the surface of Earth has not always looked as it does today. Studies of rocks and fossils, as well as the mapping of ocean floors, suggest that the continents are constantly being pushed together and moved apart. This happens very slowly over millions of years and there is no possibility that continental drift could have led to the destruction of mythical lands like Atlantis just a few thousand years ago. Even though people might hope to find hidden lands beneath the oceans, geologists do not think they will.

Chapter 5

Q *Looking again at the information you have read, why do you think there have been so many stories of lost cities that have been swallowed by the sea? Give reasons for your answer.*

A Coastlines are always changing. They are worn away by the constant pounding of the waves and can eventually crumble into the sea. Coastal cities are at risk of flooding and can be swept away if they are struck by a tsunami, as happened to the cities on the coast of Crete in Minoan times.

Chapter 6

Q *Why do you think some people believe in conspiracy theories and think that governments or organizations such as NASA might want to keep the truth from them? Give reasons for your answers.*

A A conspiracy theory is when people claim that the truth about something is being deliberately covered up. Often governments and large organizations are blamed for doing this. For some people it is more exciting to imagine that NASA is trying to cover up evidence of alien visitors on the moon than accept that a "pyramid" exists only in their imagination. With the Internet making it easy for people to share their thoughts with many others, it is not surprising that the most far-fetched ideas find believers. Always be skeptical about what other people tell you. Whenever possible, be a good mystery hunter and check the evidence for yourself.

GLOSSARY

ancestor a person or animal from whom present-day people or animals are descended

Anglo-Saxons peoples who arrived in England from Germany and Denmark in the fifth century

archaeologist someone who studies ancient ruins and artifacts

codex a type of ancient manuscript

colony a place occupied by settlers from another country

comet an icy, rocky object that orbits the sun

conspiracy theories beliefs that the truth about something is being deliberately hidden

evidence proof that something exists or is true

evolved the process by which present-day life on Earth developed from earlier life-forms

fossil the remains of a plant or animal from millions of years ago that has been preserved in rock

genetic engineering changing the characteristics of a living thing by altering its genetic code, the information found in every cell

ground-penetrating radar a device that uses radio waves to make images of underground objects

hoaxes attempts to trick someone into believing something untrue

humanoid having an appearance resembling that of a human

legend a traditional story passed down over many years

mythical based on a person, place, or event from long ago, but for which there is no actual proof

naturalist a person who studies plants and animals

novelist a writer of books of fiction

philosopher a person who studies thought and the nature of reality

physicist a scientist who studies matter, energy, motion, and force

Romano-British part of the culture that developed in Britain while it was under Roman rule

sacred holy and deserving respect

Sanskrit an ancient Indian language

scripture holy writings

sonar a device for detecting objects underwater using sound waves

species a group of living things that look similar and can reproduce

tsunami a giant wave, often caused by an earthquake or eruption

zoologist a person who studies animals

FOR MORE INFORMATION

BOOKS

Down, David. *The Archaeology Book* (Wonders of Creation). Green Forest, AR: Master Books, 2010.

Hyde, Natalie. *The Lost City of Atlantis.* New York, NY: Crabtree Publishing, 2016.

Karst, Ken. *Enduring Mysteries: Atlantis.* Mankato, MN: Creative Paperbacks, 2015.

Miner Huey, Lois. *The Search for El Dorado* (Totally True Adventures). New York: Random House Books, 2016.

WEBSITES

Discover more about archaeology on the website of the American Museum of Natural History:
www.amnh.org/explore/ology/archaeology

Read legends and facts about El Dorado:
www.ancient.eu/El_Dorado

Discover more about the ancient Maya:
www.q-files.com/history/aztec-inca-maya

Check out what is really going on in space on NASA's website:
www.nasa.gov

INDEX